Ice Swimmers

Written by Sarah O'Neil

Flying Start
to Literacy®

T0363498

Contents

Introduction

In the summer, many people like to swim in the sea or in swimming pools.

When winter comes, most people swim in heated indoor pools. But some people like to swim in lakes and seas that are frozen.

These people are called ice swimmers.

In Canada and the USA, ice swimmers are called the Polar Bears.

Ice swimmers in Russia are known as the Walruses.

Chapter 1: Getting ready
Ice pools

Ice swimmers cut holes in the ice that covers lakes or the sea to make ice pools Ice swimmers swim in these pools.

The water in ice pools is usually a little warmer than freezing, but the air can be much colder.

Some ice pools are quite small – just the right size for people to jump into. Others are as big as small swimming pools and people can swim around in them.

In larger pools, ice swimmers get into the water by climbing down a ladder.

What ice swimmers wear

Most ice swimmers wear the same swimwear they would wear when swimming in summer.

Many ice swimmers also wear woollen hats when they are swimming. This helps to keep their body heat in and protects their heads from the very cold air.

Ice swimmers wear sandals to protect their feet from the ice as they walk to the water.

Chapter 2: Ice cold water Swimming

In small ice pools, people usually jump in, tread water for a few minutes and then get out. In larger pools, they swim around.

Ice swimmers usually keep their heads out of the water when they are swimming so they do not get too cold. If people's bodies get too cold, they can die. Most ice swimmers do not stay in the water longer than 15 minutes.

Swimming under ice

Sometimes people swim in the water under the ice. Two holes are cut in the ice. Ice swimmers jump into one hol and swim all the way to the other hole.

After swimming

After swimming in ice pools, all
ice swimmers must warm their bodies
up again. If they don't get warm,
they can become very sick.

Some ice swimmers warm up by spending
time in a heated room called a sauna.
Other ice swimmers take a hot shower or
sit in a spa to warm up.

spa

sauna

14

Ice swimmers enjoy warming their
bodies up after being so cold. It makes
their bodies feel fantastic.

Chapter 3:
Breaking records
Ice swimming races

There are ice swimming races in many parts of the world. The world championships of ice swimming are held each year in ice pools that are 25 metres long. These pools are cut into the ice on lakes.

People start the race in the water. They must swim breaststroke so that their heads stay above the water and do not get wet.

Many swimmers enter these races each year.

Swimming under ice

The world record for swimming the longest distance under the ice is held by Wim Hof. He swam over 50 metres under the ice.

Wim Hof also holds the world record for the longest ice bath.

Wim Hof

Swimming in the coldest water

Lewis Pugh holds the world record for swimming in the coldest water.

Lewis Pugh swam one kilometre in the water at the North Pole. He swam for just over 18 minutes in the freezing cold water. No other person has ever done this before.

Lewis Pugh has an unusual skill.
He is able to make his body get warmer
just by thinking about it!

Conclusion

Swimming in ice pools is not something that all people like to do. But ice swimmers say that it is a fantastic sport that makes you feel good.

Index